Dad's Dancing Decorators

Level 9 – Gold

Helpful Hints for Reading at Home

The graphemes (written letters) and phonemes (units of sound) used throughout this series are aligned with Letters and Sounds. This offers a consistent approach to learning whether reading at home or in the classroom.

HERE ARE SOME COMMON WORDS THAT YOUR CHILD MIGHT FIND TRICKY:

water	where	would	know	thought	through	couldn't
laughed	eyes	once	we're	school	can't	our

TOP TIPS FOR HELPING YOUR CHILD TO READ:

- Encourage your child to read aloud as well as silently to themselves.
- Allow your child time to absorb the text and make comments.
- Ask simple questions about the text to assess understanding.
- Encourage your child to clarify the meaning of new vocabulary.

This book focuses on developing independence, fluency and comprehension. It is a gold level 9 book band.

Dad's Dancing Decorators

Written by
Hermione Redshaw

Illustrated by
Irene Renon

Dad's new flat was boring and grey. It was very clean and tidy, and big enough for each of his three daughters, Chloe, Amelia and Bryony, to have their own room. However, all the girls would do was sit.

"Time to do something about this!" thought Dad.

He took an old radio out of a box, placed it on the table and switched it on. Bryony looked first, and when she giggled, Chloe and Amelia looked over, too. Dad was dancing – the strangest of dances, shuffling along to a jazzy tune filled with all sorts of vibrant instruments all at once.

"Come on, girls!" said Dad energetically. "On your feet!"

Bryony jumped off the sofa, eager to start dancing to the music herself. Then, Dad handed her a paint brush.

"What's this?" asked Bryony.
"We're going to decorate the flat!" said Dad.

Chloe and Amelia exchanged uncertain looks. Bryony, too, seemed unsure.
"But, Dad," said Chloe, "we don't know how to decorate."
"I'll teach you," said Dad.

First, Dad got them to change into some old clothes. "Now it doesn't matter if you get splattered with paint!" he said.

Dad gave them each a wall and a tin of paint. He showed Chloe how to use a small brush to paint around doors and switches. Then, he showed Amelia how to use a roller so she could paint big bits of the wall in seconds.

Bryony sat on Dad's shoulders to paint the top of her wall, bobbing her head as Dad swayed, moving them both to the music. Chloe and Amelia soon started tapping their feet and wiggling their hips, too!

"Oh, no!" said Amelia. She was looking at Chloe's wall, then Bryony's, then Dad's. "We've painted each wall a different colour!"

It was true. They had a red wall, a yellow wall, a green wall and a blue wall – and the kitchen had somehow been splattered purple.

"Not to worry!" said Dad. He twirled each of his daughters under his arm. Colours flew this way and that, splattering across the walls and leaving big paint splodges on the furniture. Let's not mention the mess it made of Dad, Chloe, Amelia and Bryony.

When they stood back, they admired their rainbow living area.
"Much better!" said Dad, and the girls had to agree.

Next weekend, it was time to paint Bryony's room.

Dad placed the radio on the windowsill. Once the girls were in their painting clothes, Dad turned the radio on.

A drum beat. This time, there was no delay. Instantly, the three girls started tapping their feet and armed themselves with their brushes.

Bryony took the lead, splashing green and yellow across the walls as she jumped around. Chloe followed her, adding long, flowing strokes of brown in confident leaps. Dad watched as shapeless blobs transformed into trees. He was distracted as Amelia ran past, dashing and dotting black on the walls to the rhythm of the drumming. When his eyes found the wall again, animal faces stared back at him from between leaves and branches.

Chloe, Amelia and Bryony were surprised when they stepped back. They had been transported into a vibrant JUNGLE. Giraffes poked their heads through thick, green leaves. Cheetahs peered through glistening grass. Toucans perched on delicate vines.

Dad pitched a tent over Bryony's bed. That evening, they ate their dinner on a picnic rug in the middle of the room.

After that, came Amelia's room. The girls focused so hard that they managed to paint the whole room dark blue with hardly any mess. Something was wrong, though.

"Dad!" Amelia exclaimed suddenly. "You forgot to turn on the music!"
"Yes! Get the radio, get the radio!" cried Chloe and Bryony.
So, he did.

The sounds that came from the radio were chiming and warbly. As the music swelled, Amelia felt the sudden urge to spin quickly on the spot. She had forgotten she was holding a paintbrush dripping in white paint! The specks of white on the deep blue looked like stars in space, and the chimes in the music gave them a twinkle.

"I just remembered something!" said Dad, and he dashed from the room.

Dad returned with an old tin of glow-in-the-dark paint.

"Ooooh!" the girls said together.

As the music swelled, the colours flowed from Chloe and Bryony's brushes. They created constellations and galaxies, rockets and even an astronaut, all while Amelia and Dad worked on making the stars glow.

When they had finished, they did not admire their work in the light. Dad made the room as dark as possible and they gazed up at OUTER SPACE. Amelia climbed to the top of her loft bed.

"I can touch the stars!" she said gleefully.

Chloe's room caused arguments among the sisters. Chloe wanted to boss the others around to make sure everything would end up perfect. Amelia and Bryony just wanted to have fun. The song playing on the radio today was no good, either. It was as loud and screechy as the girls' fighting.

Finally, Chloe threw a cushion at Amelia. Amelia ducked, letting it fly past to hit Bryony. Bryony fell and knocked half a tin of white paint all over the bottom of the nicely painted walls.

"Oops!" said Bryony, and she started using the cushion to mop up the mess.

That's when Dad changed the radio channel. The new song was too light and soft to argue over. "Like a cloud," Bryony said. If a song could sound like a cloud, this song certainly did, but what Bryony was actually talking about was the paint on the wall.

Chloe's cushions became a painting tool as useful as a brush. They danced with graceful, ballet-like movements, blotting the splashed white into the other colours.

Dad's glow-in-the-dark paint was not needed. The clouds on the walls seemed to glow on their own, as though the Sun was really behind them.

Dad found the fluffiest white rug to add to the middle of the room, and Chloe now had plenty of white cushions to add to her bed.

Standing in Chloe's room now felt like standing on a cloud beneath a fresh sky.

The only room left untouched was Dad's room.
"It's fine as it is, really," Dad tried to insist.
"Nonsense!" said Amelia.
"We'll make it nice for you!" said Bryony.

As Dad picked up his paint brush, Chloe took
it off him. "Don't worry," she said. "You
sit down and have a cup of tea. We'll sort
everything!"

Dad watched the girls dance away into his room, and back out and back in as they collected more and more paints and tools. He could hear the radio and the girls singing a breezy, care-free song. Dad, however, was not care-free. He had to admit he was a little worried.

"All finished!" said Chloe, beaming as she, Amelia and Bryony came out of the room. Their clothes were covered in more colours than the rainbow living room and they were beaming proudly. Amelia was careful to shut the door before Dad could sneak a peek at the room.

"We're going to need a blindfold," said Amelia firmly.

As they did not have anything to hand, they used Bryony, piggy backing on Dad's back with her hands over his eyes. Chloe and Amelia held his hands and guided Dad into the room. Dad heard the click of the door as it opened and the clunk as it closed behind them.

The girls said, "Three ... two ... one!"

At first, Dad thought nothing had changed. The walls were still grey. There was no mess. Had he been tricked?

Then, he turned his head.

Across one wall was a large mural of Dad, Chloe, Amelia and Bryony, dancing with paint brushes in their hands. The girls watched Dad nervously.

"Well?" Bryony said finally. "Do you like it?"
"Like it?" said Dad, a thoughtful look on his face. "I love it!"

Dad's Dancing Decorators

1. What colour were the walls in Dad's flat?

    a) Green

    b) Black

    c) Grey

2. Which room was the first to be painted?

3. How do you think the girls felt at the start of the story while Dad's flat looked dull?

4. Why do you think Dad wanted to get the girls to start painting?

5. If you could paint your bedroom as any colour, pattern or picture, what would you choose?

©2022 **BookLife Publishing Ltd.**
King's Lynn, Norfolk, PE30 4LS, UK

ISBN 978-1-80155-808-2

All rights reserved. Printed in Poland.
A catalogue record for this book is available
from the British Library.

Dad's Dancing Decorators
Written by Hermione Redshaw
Illustrated by Irene Renon

An Introduction to BookLife Readers...

Our Readers have been specifically created in line with the London Institute of Education's approach to book banding and are phonetically decodable and ordered to support each phase of Letters and Sounds.

Each book has been created to provide the best possible reading and learning experience. Our aim is to share our love of books with children, providing both emerging readers and prolific page-turners with beautiful books that are guaranteed to provoke interest and learning, regardless of ability.

BOOK BAND GRADED using the Institute of Education's approach to levelling.

PHONETICALLY DECODABLE supporting each phase of Letters and Sounds.

EXERCISES AND QUESTIONS to offer reinforcement and to ascertain comprehension.

BEAUTIFULLY ILLUSTRATED to inspire and provoke engagement, providing a variety of styles for the reader to enjoy whilst reading through the series.

AUTHOR INSIGHT:
HERMIONE REDSHAW

Hermione Redshaw has been writing books for over eight years, with a passion for adventure and fantasy. Her writing is often distinguished by themes of family and personal growth. Hermione holds a Bachelor's degree in English Language, Communication and Linguistics, with a keen interest in communicating difficult ideas in a clear and accessible way. Her Master's in Children's Publishing focused Hermione's experiments with bold and innovative concepts, from story apps to dyslexia-friendly and educational adventures. She joins BookLife Publishing with a drive to engage new and old readers alike.

This book focuses on developing independence, fluency and comprehension. It is a gold level 9 book band.